The Kangaroo Girl

The Kangaroo Girl

poems by

JUDITH BAUMEL

Judith Baumel, The Kangaroo Girl
© 2011 Judith Baumel

First edition, May 2011

ISBN: 978-0-9823594-3-3
Printed and bound in the USA
Library of Congress Control Number: 2010942800

Cover Photo: Abraham Baumel

for my family—Abe, Betty, Sara, Ellis

Contents

Photo Of Author In Kangaroo Pajamas

(Macombs Road, The Bronx)

The Kangaroo girl will not be written,
$\qquad$ refuses to be written.
The Kangaroo girl will not be recovered,
$\qquad$ refuses to be recovered.
The Kangaroo girl, crumpled, tearing
at the folds, peeling at the corners
in a wallet forty years
will not be re—

$\qquad$ refuses to be.
Fingers splayed, her right hand pulls a blur
from out of her plane,
$\qquad$ which energy is her refusal to be re—
vised/visited/vamped/versed.
All else—crisp static half-dollar
eyes, the never-ironed cotton,
antiquely crumpled, perky ears
on her hooded head—
is alert to the silvering light.
From refuse in the dark, father,
thrusting, poking, stirring,
emulsions,
made her. Emersed, emergent,

$\qquad$ effulgent.

There was the pocket through which
she came to the emended dimension
across the gloss. Across the dross of years
the square tipped four fingers and thumb did—
the shaking hand did—
haul herself to a new hand, did—
vanquish or varnish, did—
harden the view/the voice/the verse.

Hem Stitch Hemi Stichs

Its primary virtues

           are the subtlety that makes

it nearly invisible,

           picking the barest piece

of cloth, parting

           mercerized threads,

and the wonderful way

           it doubles back

does everything twice.

           In the years I was learning

the stitch I was also

           being told by the school

librarian to do everything

           twice—read

each book, of course,

           but she also pushed

personal hygiene,

           hand washing,

nail brushing.

           The stitch doubles

back building

           flexibility and play

across the fabric,

           the vectors of tension

form back and forth

           and up and down,

so the hem hews

           to any human

pull or push.

           Never have I seen

this stitch on garments

    other than ones

she made and ones

    I make with this twice-as-long

step. Strength.

    Firmness. Insurance.

All her nearly

    cubical clothes

given away

    at death, those drops

of magic made

    from scraps—

for her short full chest

    and tank-like torso

she'd build a dress

    from her customers' leftovers,

the wardrobe augmented

    on whims the way

I cook kasha

    because I have a taste for it.

Beside her I had a strict

    apprenticeship

of no teaching.

    Watching. Imitating.

After she lost

    her eye I'd thread

the needle or pick

    at black fabrics

she couldn't manage.

    All the dresses are gone.

Did she really hem

    this way or have

I invented the pattern

            to repeat as a periodic

memory of mercers

            we'd bargain bolts with.

The fabric across my lap,

            the needle shallowing

into a single strand,

            picking it apart,

drawing the thread

            through and back,

forcing this

            as she insisted my inheritance,

her first granddaughter

            balabusta

a real balabusta

            house wife.

Wanton waning

            wistful arts

I can't shake out of my hands.

Generator

Did you imagine my belly the Van de Graaff generator
you built in the bedroom of your adolescent
experiments? A low steady current
spread across the dome, exciting
and not at all. Variable.
High voltage, low current drawing
the hand and communicating no pulse.
Was there no impulse, that summer?
For me there was the little furnace of that baby
in the summer heat so oppressive we could hardly
walk the dog, and then the ordinary heat
of all that extra blood through me.
I burned so hot all those months.
I burned in the suburban smog,
I burned at the sight of you,
I burned at the edges of my fingers,
the wet backs of my knees and their chafing fat,
I burned, and corners of my eyes learned
their involuntary release, a tear trickle
from the outer corner, tracking
a jagged sign down my cheek like
the harmless lightning on the generator's globe.
I burned to breathe the carbon dioxide
of your exhalations,
the oxygen of your imprecations.
I burned. Believe me. Do.
And to you, what was it, from the outside,
what was it to your cool cool hand,
while I burned?

The Influence Of Peers

I don't want to hear that kind of language in this house
Try shoot shucks sugar
sheleileigh Shalala,
anything but the vowel
which hits the iffy one
and comes too close.
I'm an idiot has taken over,
though not for long.
I've ceded ground on butt,
the lost tuchas, tush, tushy
having had the double virtues of ethnic
reminder and gentle enjoyment
of the soft yielding place
from which I wiped with care
that which I wish to hear
called only by cuteness, or evoked.
Well, what could he do,
my muscular ball of opposition,
that whirl of destruction,
wielding Hrunting,
tossing chairs and books
and punching out the wind
behind him screaming
beep you beep you beep you beep.

"Rampant Hippocamp"

Quod Severis Metes

It is time to reach back, touch it, understand it,

It is time to reach back, touch it, understand it,

touch it, understand it, live it, know it,
though it may be merely memory curling-in on itself,

may be the sea horse curling its tail beneath itself,
the Coptic textile restitching for the Christian Nile
a broad-tape roundel of briefly fabulous myth.

In the Lover's Lane of the fabulous Bliss gardens
I said I was remembering the amphitheater's oval pool
—memorizing it—you corrected. I meant I was
forcing the autumnal reflections of the trees
through my hippocampus into my processed thought.

We thought different things when we saw that phrase
typed on a display tag in the late-Egyptian room,
our shoes on the hunt mosaic floor of wild men
skewering boar, lion, a tigress they'd pursued
and defeated in agony. You knew it was a small spiral
in the brain, that it was the brain's loyal file clerk,
retentive librarian, efficient general contractor.
I knew other shapes such a creature takes.

There are no words for the furious ride
you then took, whipping your temper beside me, far
far out and away. You refused to take my side.

You would not go back with me over the terrible years
but insisted in each breath's instant; would not name
places we knew, would not touch my old or my new skin,
but said particular, temporizing, temporal phrases
meant to stir the air of now, and then evaporate.
I have kept them stored. If we were to remember
forgiveness, we would need to trust the next word: Love,
the only way we might find the next word, is to have
heard it before, and reach back, touch it, understand.

To A Middle-Aged Suicide

Your hand came from the sleeping bag on the floor
in the dark to my thigh. I returned it to you, returned
it, you remembered, "with compassion gently."
Thirty years later, your hand went up my skirt

—"with compassion" would be a nice chiasmus
but it was just your habit to perform
vulgarity; we laughed together. I'd learned
to make our annual greetings a baroque

pain ceremony; to recast those pricks,
humiliations, confusions. To modulate
discomfort, and accept, reject, mull, chew,
your gotten-over bravado, a posturing

beneath which something—what?—crept into place.
You are not dead *to* me but dead *in* life.

Notes For The Elegy

Without	Not yet
But	Still
Because	Unless
Despite	After
However	Within

Your friends—good talkers—all
admiration of your talk.

It was the silences I heard, how we
become most ourselves at our boundaries.

In the surrounding silence remain
we who do have rights in the matter—

not those late devolving lovers—
tongues cleft to palates.

Body betrays brilliant will
your last quaking quip taught.

A kiss, not yours, at your street corner.
Flesh of lips answered,

muscles of fingers stretched the skin—
that yielding organ—learning.

In all the days of my life since—
in all the nights of my life since—

each since a workbook of exercises;
the habit, bad, good, is put on daily.

Monteverde

we felt like frontiersmen, and everything we picked up was new
and something different
—Nalini Nadkarni

How the fog comes across the canopy
bringing Saharan sand.
How the moss mat rebuilds the world
above the shadows.
How where we walk is disconnected,
is replaced,
is what we chase. How it feeds
the earth's lungs.
How a lithe gibbon flashes inward,
a deliberate
orangutan weighs shortcuts
in the canopy's branch
highways, a fledgling harpy eagle,
begun as white fluff
feeding on the sloth mother brought,
rehearses wing span,
builds a lethal eye, aiming beakish sharpness
or is it sharp beakishness . . .

In Memory Of Douglas Cameron Gordon

(Tsangpo River, Tibet)

The sun came up, was gone
—rain, storm, uncertainly filled air—
and then it set.
And again. And again.
Nothing unusual.
You went then into white
water and again and again.
So many times so distant
from the short time we made time,
and you took care,
took care of me.
Then it was always about weather
and since, about weather, passing
the building your father lived in
and, on the other coast,
your mother. I'd think
of you, more of the years,
between. Into white water. So for me,
what difference? A spirit or a spirit.
In a land of spirit flags,
your name flutters in the brief sun.

Monumental Grief

At last, this is the poem about your monument scarf.

About the monument scarf you've been waving

At me ever since that afternoon twenty years ago
Clare gave it to you in the Andover house, freezing

As it would be even in early fall, and she tossed
that piece of silk to you, it had been
Pooh's, from the heaps of family archaeology.

About the monument scarf with its scenes
of Rome that only later I would come to love
as I would love the old Italian magazines scattered
in all the rooms of the place, almost not at all a house
someone lived in, but some post-diluvial storehouse.

About the monument scarf you see
as a fitting—what—Metaphor. Trope.
Allusion. Apostrophe. Symbol. Image. Entree
into the story of your family
which anyway you're doing as a novel,
so I'm to take this pale green square
scarf and build from it something square
and lyrical, regular, right and true.
About the monument scarf you wore
to her memorial service when, at the party
after, one last long grand chaotic Sunday Lunch,
I saw you in the kitchen as I sat in a dark
room meditating on the intervening twenty years.

About that head scarf I saw fluttering brightly
in a bright room across the distance
of corridors as if it were a movie or a strong
dream. I'd driven to New Hampshire in morning
darkness and ended the day in darkness
on a couch surrounded by dark
things and dark thoughts and dark years
and so many of the things I've let go—

The ones I had swiftly waved away and the ones
I clutched at desperately dragging them back.
There I sat in the dark holding onto the corporeal
flesh of the disappeared in a dream,
knowing the way I had seen Clare collect and pursue,
pile up what she wanted was characteristically pure,
knowing I've never regretted saving, even as I lived
in the painful mess that accumulating means.
Knowing I've felt as a physical force the rebuke
of what I've passed over. There I sat holding the hair
and the skin and the muscle of what I'd let go,
murmuring over it as if to coax it back to me
and in that waving scarf were monuments—
Il Colosseo, I Fori, Il Circo Massimo—structures in ruins,
not least of which was my life, since what had come back
had done so briefly, only to remind me of the empty room
that this clutter would soon become, this house
I'd never revisit—a monument a stone a headstone
over earth filled with the active life that is destruction,
with the life that breaks down our own residue,
with the equivocating soil in which we will ultimately rest.

Servomechanics

That was the year I lived on Linnaean Street
and tried to put the chaos of my life in order.

I'd jog past Vanserg, down to the rhinos
in the courtyard of the Bio Labs,

go out beneath Blaschka's glass flowers
—their sturdy bohemian crystal bonds—,

through The Yard, Eliot House, the Bridge,
between the B-School and the Stadium

—which summer was The Bacchae
with live sheep there?—

to swim the new pool whose engineers
had mastered wave feedback. Dry,

I'd jog back up through the Busch Reisinger,
—nodding to tuxedoed Max Beckmann—,

and past the Observatory, to Walden
Pond—never far enough from anything

to make retreat more than its own conceit.
—Why have even one chair when we have the ground?—

and home, where, inside, that winter,
my amaryllis came up, bitter Tiresias,

all penetrating bud until it opened
like a trumpet of belladonna

and then shriveled to pink grey labia,
four dull inward-folded pieces.

I longed for it to stay just so for—ever.
So I nipped the top and killed the plant

and put upon my desk a life study
of that which prefers to refuse,

self-made memento mori, powdery, item
against the Latin nomenclature,

against the many means of classification
I trucked with every day,

all that brain power, tinned and tabled and tidy,
while I couldn't, while I couldn't choose.

You Take An Onion

As if at a quilting bee or coffee klatsch,
the women talk around
their children's frightful wheezing out
and grabbing in through ventilators
that keep them alive:
You take an onion and chop it fine
and some honey and pepper and mix
it in a sock and wear it all night;
you warm some rolled-up undershirts,
not clean and best left sweaty,
in a frying pan and put them on the chest.
Who among them really believed
she'd make a creature
so disabled by the very air around
him that this would be the weekly drill?
In which of the cubicles down the pediatric
ER, dioramas of loneliness and news
and doubt and wonder and wait,
is the mother who considered that
the very blood running through
her child's arteries would fight itself so hard
it would build passages stenotic with fibroids?
Did any one lie in bed under the pressure
of her growing belly and dream through the panic
of an unusual stillness so many cells growing wild
outside herself? Or wake from a dream
where her child slips out of her so early
he is blind and deaf and naked
even of skin, and think it was truth
enough to give up hope? Did the one who

found the maleness of her newborn boy
so alien that for months she held him
to her breast as if he were the flesh of a lost
lonesome part requiring reattachment,
conceive this isolation, the dumb clicks and beeps
and rumbles of the machines,
while down the hall, the homey asthma room
fills with the remedies of grandmothers.
Children wired and tubed through a disdain
of modern medicine,
women share their recipes:
you take an onion,
you take a shirt.

New Hampshire Inventory

Only venison in the freezer.
Curry venison on the stove plate—
curry made the meat palatable
when I would still eat that sort of thing.
Borrowed cross country skis on a full
moon night, moving as if on borrowed
legs, when my friends house-sat for a new
dance company. Used the sponsor's towels
and soaps. Everything was Calvin Klein.
That August we harvested, rushing,
the company's cash crop at midnight
because a neighbor kid saw someone
strange sniffing around the good dope plants.
Calluses from dragging stalks through woods,
stripping, drying them in batches all
the perfumed night in a gas oven.
So many small tip leaves I stole when
I still smoked that sort of thing. I thought
I'd forgotten the subset threesome
we had formed years before New Hampshire.
The dancers would link their bodies like
a single fungus projected large
to our cool eyes. With centrifugal
force they linked against logic, confused
order and desire, the way we had done
when I was so young I didn't get
that sort of thing and hated our friends
who called me bad, transformed me into
the one who led him away, the prod
in her side, the single disruptive

force. He loved my hair; I had her chop
it off. I felt so soft, when I still
could manage to feel that sort of thing.
Somehow, the larger group kept going,
all of us in changing pairs around
that shaky couple. We'd drive up north,
their new place sealed warm against winter's
isolating cold with venison
and dope. The deep core inside me like
a solenoid, unchanging in my
change, iron in my fluctuations.
Still willing to do that sort of thing,
I let him drag me to an upstairs
bedroom in the dark so he could play
guitar and sing, with no irony,
"Go Away Little Girl." I couldn't
drive then so I had to wait the night
for my ride to pack and hit the road.
And it was over. Yet year after
year after year my journal pages
prove how little changed as I grew up.
Though I found much more polish, and I
stopped that sort of nonsense, the coil
remained wrapped the same way long beyond
that last drive back, humiliated
and laughing, the plunger waiting for
a low current to flow through, descend,
and quietly ignite the big one.

The Letter

looking at Vermeer and Cogniet

The rectangle frames a world
full of light whiteness right
angles corners
the face confronts the air
the face splits the difference
of one eye in and one eye out of
the letter he's come to disrupt
the future to remind
the past to promise
the now to break
the old promises the new
all changed in an instant
changed not least ambition
the map informs at large
a larger world in the square
the empty mind like
the empty billet
waste of walls on which
a guitar is hung
and all is green spreading
all is white all is golden
there is a sun beyond
a shuttered window in
the letter is not
the passage through
is not the window.
How deeply I believe I see through it.

Snow-Day

What was it drove me to insist on sleds,
to pull the children out of the playground
and toward the park's much steeper hills, instead
of making angels? I was waist deep and bound
by ice, and they were too. In their eyelashes
was unremovable ice. They crawled and flailed
on snow. The progress of their grudging limbs
slow. Surely memory of snow-fort caches,
the childish city happily derailed,
its hopes of milk and bread and papers dim.

When I was young I came to Boston late
late late one winter night from Baltimore.
The pre-dawn, post-blizzard of seventy-eight
glowed in the silent town where dump trucks bore
their loads of snow as through a secret city—
filling and then dumping in the harbor,
filling yet again. I'd just removed
a child from my womb. Well someone else did it
and it was not a child but some small scar
inside. It meant nothing to me, that newt,

that early fetus, and the procedure meant
nothing except perhaps the end of fear
and queasiness. Today how I resent
the way sadness and loss are souvenirs
we're forced to carry with us. Listen—Happy
is the way I felt, and still I feel,
when I can shovel through the euphemisms

of those who speak for me. More happy. Happy
that forever will that speck, that organism
remain forever small and unfulfilled

in contrast to my son who came exactly
ten years after to the day, and to
a woman ready for him. I had wept
returning to my now-lost lover anew,
seeing the streets of Boston being cleaned,
scraped clear of the invading snow
that clung to arteries, that fairly smothered
our chance to try to make a normal flow
of life. That struggle with the midnight gleam:
the wiping, tidying gesture of a mother.

Mr. Goldfish And Vicky

Of the days when Sam fell in love
with Vicky, this scene remains:
his legs draped over Julia's Windsor chair,
Vicky in his lap, his nose to her
snout as she licked him. We left her
and a portion of Sam's heart at Hedges,
to roam Sumerside in the village
of Buckland near Faringdon, Gloucestershire,
all her Border Collie genes
intent on ingathering, keeping together,
reckoning and accounting, a kind of canine
Shire Reeve, and returned to our
Bronx high-rise, its great distant
views of hospitals and armories and bridges
and its no-dog clause in the proprietary lease.

And thus enters Mr. Goldfish,
one of a pair in a carnival prize,
who came home to an icy bowl of Dis,
to a refusal to name, or make
comfortable. His companion died
but this nameless fish survived,
growing first to the job title
Goldfish, then to the respectful Mr.
All night reading, I hear his moods.
The ravenous picks at the surface
of the oxygen-poor water, the turns
in the current of boredom, the way
he begs me for something, makes me worry
for his weight, worry for love,
for his limited, fishy, pathetic love.

Winchester

for James, Elizabeth, Thomas and Catherine Yarrow

a.

Anno igitur ab incarnatione Domini
mo co lxxxo ixo, Clemens papa
Richard, the son of King Henry II by Eleanor,
and brother of King Henry III was hallowed
King of the English by Baldwin
Archbishop of Canterbury
at Westminster on 3 September.

When James was four, he and I discussed
cosmology at Herschel's house
and I imagined the transit of love
coming in and out of James's life
like a bird of legend with a magic seed.

b.

It caused many people to whisper and to marvel
when a bat was seen flying through the monastery
at midday, although the day was clear,
circling about in an untimely way,
especially about the king's throne.

My dears, old fond hopes have escaped
me, slipped out of my hand, wings,
beak, feathers, all, past those stone gates
on College Street where I now find you,
past where Izaac Walton and Jane Austen died,
where James has burrowed into chambers
and sits beneath the subtle glass of the cloister
chapel, as a classical scholar—these things
close to my heart and distant.

c.

On that same coronation day,
at about the hour of that solemnity
in which the Son was immolated
to the Father, they began in the city of London
to immolate the Jews to their father, the Devil.
It took them so long to celebrate this mystery
that the holocaust was barely completed
on the second day. The other towns and cities
of the country emulated the faith
of the Londoners, and with equal devotion
they dispatched their bloodsuckers bloodily to hell.

Richard Coeur de Lion may have protected
the Jews of the town, but you know how
that old confusing convenient connection
between the kings and their financiers turns
quickly inside out like an empty sow's purse,
you know Simon of Monfort goes after the king
by going after the Jews, huzzah,
and the Winton twenty-four who attempted
to protect the Jews on Shoemaker Street.
You find shoemakers thick in the irony
of the Swithun monk, Richard of Devises,
whose chronicle called the place the Jerusalem
of these parts, reports the blood libel,
and takes swipes at all the other English towns.

d.

You kids asked me once "what do you believe?"
I answered something complex and long-winded,
and found out later you meant simply
little things like Jesus or transubstantiation,
those most simplest of things no one taught
you even in England's best schools.

To some degree, but not everywhere
the same, this storm against the incorrigible
people raged throughout the kingdom.
Winchester alone spared its worms.

e.

Those post coronation riots
continued north to York in March 1190.
While William that Norman usurper and his kin
loved the Jews and set them up:
a synagogue on Scowrtenestret,
near the king's gaol, businesses,
rights to the St. Giles's Fair,
rights, occasional, to the civic life.
Or needed them so badly—their calm
medical practice, their willingness
to trade, travel, lend, mint. How well
the Norman kings kept visceral
disgust at the necessary Jew
at bay while he financed
the crusades to rid the world
of the eastern heathens. Can you
parse my irony or my disgust?

f.

They were a prudent and farsighted
people and a city that always behaved
in a civilized manner. They never did anything
over-hastily, for fear they might repent
of it later and they looked to the end
of things rather than to the beginnings.
They did not want partially to vomit
forth the undigested mass violently
and at their peril, even though they were urged
to do so, when they were not ready.
They hid it in their bowels modestly
(or naturally) dissimulating their disgust
meanwhile, till at an opportune time
for remedies they could cast out
all the morbid matter once and for all.

By which our dear Richard
of Devises means 18 July 1290 under Edward.
I carried James, my godson,
to a baptismal font in Oxford
over the objections of Father Michael,
promising dedication by
saying my people wouldn't want him.
Now here in Winchester, down the High Street,
past Jewry Street and the Buttercross,
I release him, as he releases me
of obligation.

g.

And nearly as if my own flesh
—but isn't part of my pleasure
in all of you, that your blond Saxon
faces and flesh couldn't be my flesh—
note my excited snobbish pride
in James, Wykamist,
with his notions and his toy in chambers,
the trusty sweater, the three-volume vocabulary
of the school reaching back very far
and also very far forward to power.

h.

I can't parse the cheerful sarcasm
of Chaucer when he repeats Devises's tale
in the Prioress, of the murdered boy,
or Devises's own late-Latin sarcasm
dismissing London, Canterbury,
Lincoln, Ely, Oxford, Exeter refreshing
both men and beasts with the same provender,
and on unto Winchester, with such Christian
Christians that the Jew would go there
to be Christian among them.

i.

Can you explain how it is the flesh-
and-blood Jew becomes the theological Jew,
the Judensau, sorcerer, goat, horned
demonic pig, serpentine usurer,
blood-spattered poisoner? Explain
not that we were needed
but that we might have been tolerated,
not that the white cloaked clerical hermit
stood at the base of William's Castle in York
and chanted that the enemies be crushed,
but that the soft-hearted Richard
might have found a way to protect us?

j.

Never mind. Don't bother
with any of the above;
those are tired old questions.
I need to answer my own,
my own people's willingness
to compromise and not, to go on and not,
to bend and blend and not,
to see the Swithun monk's Jews, ever zealous,
after the Jewish fashion, for the honor
of their city, so that when perfectly ordinary
modern Jews look to black Hasidic hat,
to the haredi for the purity
of preservation, I wonder how they think
we have survived, how they make sense
of the Haftorah, the crypto Jews,
the maranos, hidden mezzuzot,
Cincinnati seminaries, self-stopping elevators.

k.

Am I making any sense?

If Winchester can train James,
ah, well, then it also can train me.

Misericordia

When the Sinatra brothers blew off

a bunch of fingers, two thumbs, and one

eyeball among them one July 3
mishandling fireworks it seemed good—

a finally successful payback (the first try
having been merely burning out the garage
and mother-in-law apartment

of their house on our block) for the two
bicycles, one sled, and one watch they'd taken
from my brother over the years. I don't
want to talk about revenge or the compact
feeling of goodness that is the consolation

of the meek daily facing small tortures but that
they'd been brought to Misericordia
Hospital where all the Catholics went. The Jews
went to Jacobi or Montefiore, and we lived,
these two threads, amid each other
in a great childish confusion, unable to beat
the weft to the warp. I can imagine the informal
lectures the Catholic kids received, as I recall

mine about heartless popes and the persistent mimicry
of the New Testament. In fact, I'd heard the echoes
of what they heard when Charles Cutaia, who "liked" me,
said he felt sorry for me one lunch period and followed
that with an afternoon in which he pointed, Ruth-like,
to the far wall of the school yard and said "for Judy!"

so that when, at the next pitch, he actually hit
the home run, I had to run home in at least three
states of embarrassment. The Sinatra brothers
went to a hospital I imagined would culture
more misery for them. From the building's tower the word
hung over the Bronx River Parkway, and driving past
I never hesitated to consider the misery within.

When did the Catholic kids learn the meaning
of the word? During "Released Time," those leisurely
Wednesday afternoons when they went to catechism
and the Jewish kids wandered the half empty classroom
a little happy, a little lonely?
Did they know that misery develops with one
in need of mercy? Or somehow through
indulgences of food, or a small bench grinning
at your knees with the cynical knowledge of sin
embedded in a gargoyle's smirk along the pew?
Or that what is at the heart of the word is the heart
and its ability, with its up and down, in and out,
to grant mercy and then remove it, endlessly?
So I later learned reading Benito Pérez Galdós's *Misericordia*,
the last of his novelas contemporáneas
where the moral rightness of the Madrid street
embroiders profusions of misericordia,
where the "moor" Almadena/Mordejai teaches the Sh'ma
to the saintly Benina, his Amri, as a magical formula
to achieve the riches neither can extract from their stern
patrons, casual donors and willing victims

who weave pity, compassion, and mercy for these beggars,
these petty thieves, embezzlers, happily optimistic
in their logic as they argue about who has and who doesn't,

about secret forms of loyalty and faith.
Ah, the bitter loss of the sled. That it was so easy. That
they approached us at the top of the hill, a Snow-Day,
the closed school downhill beyond us. Joey simply said "it's ours"
and it was. The hospital has shed the vestment
of its old, evocative name, and is now "Our Lady
of Mercy. " Joey and Bobby and Tony Sinatra
have undoubtedly gone on from the 600 schools,
those garbage containers for the incorrigible
in which they first found themselves judged,
heroes and villains at once, to the sort of ageless
tricks that enlivened Calle Cabeza, to the heroin
that was traded and used far out of my sight,
to the local carting or construction business
where misery is doled out in each paper-less
contract. Every Christmas we watched them set a creche,
some diminished thing along the lines of a presepe
Mrs. Sinatra must have known in her paese.
And though now, certainly, I'm sure that the Mary
they carefully placed inside the straw pitied them, I hated
her face then, hated the license it gave them, the license
it gave us to be squeamish with blood, to shirk
from those images of Mary's son, his wounds
daily displayed. My self-pity is lately transformed
as I recreate the tableau of all of us complicitous
in that old exchange—
Mrs. Sinatra lamenting her ragazzi, porca miseria,
my father who would not stoop to recover the property,
my brother ever stunned in the release of the property,
and me screaming, screaming my polite curses after
the fact—and for all of us I am now furiously without compassion.

Letter To Nando

(Henry Hudson Parkway, The Bronx)

Carissimo, I haven't forgotten your pleased
quip years ago setting foot here:

you said it was a seaside town: seaside
salt and marine light mingled in the air,

a slant, certainly, different from what I see—
the Babylonish brick kiln.

Recalled it last night retiring beneath
the fat orange harvest moon

and again when an Umbrian gold
morning limned the spines of books

piled under my eastern window.
Outside, a clear light skimmed bricks,

stones, cement, steel, of Kingsbridge, Fordham,
Soundview; it picked off one white

spot on each structure of the leaden
Bronx, tumbled from the step-streets' heights

the way it skips the tops
of white caps in the vast Atlantic

or the North Sea of the northern painters
who turned daily task into a homey optics.

From Melville's workroom window
he saw the snow-covered Berkshires

—his child-disordered house roiling below—
like the wide waste of water's

desperation in his bachelor past. I lifted my cup
of breakfast tea and for a credible instant understood

the few bright dots of light it had caught
to be holes in the bottom, and wondered

why everything I have
doesn't just drain right through that rugged sieve.

But my bucket, dear Nando, you're positive,
is solid, and still holds everything I have.

Butterwort

The soul of the wind is wind.
The wind of the soul is wind.
The breath that carries the leaf
carries the dry leaves down
the street in solitary pleas,
in mobs, that death could have undone so
many. Just to touch the wing
of the butterfly is to pull the scales
from its nervures, to pick color
from collars, to end flight.
In the dream, my dark hair came out
strand by strand, one by one, strung
with pearly nits which I hung
over my morning
head like a bead curtain
over that head from which the wiry
white renegades curled out
and the morning shook off where I'd been.

My child looked up from his pillow,
a satisfying simian scratch of his scalp
completed. He did not know
where I'd been in the dark
hours between "good" and "good."
He wanted to know from where came
to humans the very very very first louse.

The Days Of August Leapt One Over The Other

(via Birago, Perugia)

We fed the lizards bits of watermelon,
reaching from under the canvas canopy,
each lunch, to place the chunks of fruit in sun
along the terrace's concrete boundary,

and crept then back inside the tiny place
for naps, the boys in the parlor's narrow cell,
we in the bedroom, Nando reading papers
in the kitchen, soaking bread for panzanella.

Downstairs, memorials, death notices,
acknowledgments of past condolences
were plastered on the city's streets and alleys.
I learned these strangers and their families

wandering and returning.
We once outraced a hail storm, pulling
the bleaching laundry off the southern terrace.
One day at table our older son surprised

himself in accidental fluency
by asking aqua per favore, might I.
They were small gestures, small lucertole,
a green that turns to gray and back in light,

so lovely they outshone their serpent cousins,
and jostled one the other till each set
upon his fruit. Each came out furtively
and stayed in pleasure, and the boys watched in pleasure.

I'm Not Kidding

You would dismiss the comment,
wouldn't you, unless
presented with enough ironic distance
(viz. this preface),
that my son's shit smelled like heaven,
fresh mown hay, dew, new sun
on a morning-wet farm.
The first time I wiped the little
yellow brown pile, I wiped only after
enjoying its bouquet and the hospital
nurse to whom I confessed
dismissed me to my hormones.
Keeping him on my breast
exclusively couldn't maintain the smell.
He was breathing our air, suffering
our suffering; such was the corruption,
the solidification of shit, and I was busy
collecting his pieces. I didn't have the nerve
to ask for the foreskin, but the rest—
umbilical cord, hair, teeth, nail pieces,
the flaps of skin torn from life,
I was packing in labeled, ordered
envelopes, my workaday fetish.
And then came the perplexing stink
of the boys' bathroom, suggesting
another secret I had yet to learn of men.
One night I saw, in ambush, my little one,
as if on the edge of a boat
on the Nivernais canal,
drunk in closed-eye sleep,

swaying, shifting his hips
to the remembered target, hands
completely off himself, and missing,
hopelessly missing the mark.
I worry I am now missing the mark.
Missing, also, the sharp remark
you'd have had to that one's sleepy pleasure
in his efficient kidneys and extended member,
or to his brother's shriveling kidney
and the way destiny shrivels our blind intentions.
I'm missing those marks.
I'm not kidding, kiddo, not kidding,
this is only the start of how I miss you.

Electronic Allegory

The seat belt sensor.
The car door, cell phone.
alarm clock, micro-
wave. The computer,
computer printer.
The Tamagotchi.
Happy Little Egg.
My son's virtual
pet for which I have
become foster mom
when he is in school,
the way it calls me
and I respond to
its summons, urgent,
as milk released in
his infancy from
my nipples, "let-down,"
though for me it was
a cranking up of
my anxiety
and fear, as I jumped
at the cry and still
jump to the "mommy"
that sounds so different
at different ages
but the same among
same aged children. Thus
in the agora
the tone will move me
in panic before

I can distinguish
the sound's creator
or what is wanted.
It will move me toward
solution, toward what
is meant by "pushing
my buttons"
—release
and start of tension
at once —a calling.

Days Of Oak

(Monadnock, New Hampshire)

In dress clothes on the ground we sat inside
the Hampshire woods, as if a luminist canvas,
as if the very waves bringing light
to us remained without a single movement.

The tree beside you on your right dropped one
acorn at a time. A phrase, a pause,
another phrase, bulking at your shoulder
the fragments of the conversation.

From underneath the river's mirror
something urgent and alive drove up
a continuous argument of bubbles
gathering fierce and rapidly drifting.

Still still still still still.
The sun left and entered the scene, left
again the trees across the water.
The top of one tall tree shouted into fall

remarked. A maple, you said. And I said oak.
For maple you had your reasons—
one after the other, bright leaves
concealing, shadowing each other.

I was studying silence then,
training myself to stand outside myself
to watch my lips stay still, and listen, still,
it was an oak: I let you say.

The Days Of December Walked Deep Into the Backwoods

(New Bordeaux, South Carolina)

Where could he put the breathing
tube? He took a walk into old time,
old, each step, like his rain chime's
random plink, plink-plink, seizing

the moment and quieting meditation
over the piled femoral bones, or a pelt
just hidden under the brush, red and wet
with the rot of west Carolina clay,

where hunters come in season,
to strip and chop and dress and knot.
At the stone cross marking the Huguenot
church, he sought refuge in a reason

his people settled where they could make
practical appeasement, could found a school
and steal from it, merge with the Petigrus,
could slip from the war between the states,

a reason they came, *a sulon*, here,
this place, too small for a republic, too large
for an insane asylum, to forge
the gates and bars that held their chimera,

to find a way to force back the ghosts,
to liquefy and replace whatever pain

they illustrated and named, to arraign
the dybbuks and duppies with icy puff breaths.

Beside the cross, I stood at the banks of winter,
stood at the flat surface of the creek's court
from which they once drew baptismal water.
I stood at the banks of my asylum beginning.

Morphine

after May Swenson

I was a baby, a bear cub, maybe,
in his arms and held a warmth
as he set the rubber tourniquet,
outward tapping and inward tapping
inward drawing and outward drawing
the dread of what was to spread,
a single insight, a one bright light
and the shaded, shadowed cave,
anticipation, a darkened hibernation
within the muscles of that nuzzled hug.

Rowing In Eden

In the winter morning's wild—light—
that man's name—flashed—
outside his shop and memory
came—quick faucet flung—open
flooding, flushing the system
and then stillness—suppression—
of the striking hip
bone, the huge thick taut—
not like anything I'd seen
—or felt—luxury
enough—to keep me tethered
to the dark—in those days—the scotch
shimmering over ice in a squat
glass was ever the richest color—
in the room—angry angry touch
and the morning tenderness—severed—
from all that came before—the sun flickering.

Meditation In A Bright Room

Haste is the enemy. When.
In the night's damp hollow,
your hands articulating flesh,
layer by serried layer.
Haste is the enemy. Will.
Hold it silent in the mouth
each salt grain meeting
its bud's receptor.
Haste is the enemy. I.
Know that most of a day
is the sitting still,
the patient's patience.
Haste is the enemy. See.
Thumbs thread the cervical
vertebrae, thoracic, lumbar,
two, three, four. Sacrum. Coccyx.
Haste is the enemy. You.
Name the names I can't name,
find the birds in the low bush,
their shy pink answer to sun.
Haste is the enemy. When.

Who Holds You Like This?

(Jaina Figurine, Dumbarton Oaks)

Who holds you like this?
Fat tenderness, wasted desire,
upright grip on slipping cheek.
As if her arm holding his head,
her hand touching his grizzled
jaw so gently, is passion
in ready abeyance,
and his arm grasping her waist,
and his arm her thigh, diminishment.
If this is courtly love,
sun king god, moon queen courtesan,
theirs is a court of last repeated resort,
her gaze drawing light,
her arms whistling out her life.
My own arms are too tired.
Each night I go deep under,
cross to the other side of the sky,
and drag my waning shape back up.
Requiring a bow, a bracket, a brace,
requiring embrace,
I renounce my crooked arm.
I renounce my vigilant eye.
I renounce my full, my milk-full breast.

Atonement There Is Betwixt Light And Darkness

To be a we, we must include
that which we have banished—
the transgressor, the excommunicated.
Can be neither community or person
without our ex—punged, tracted parts
down to the smallest part must not
be buried without the least drop,
even if by violence we died,
scraped mopped absorbed collected
by the dedicated blessed friends.
This day, each portion of our confession
comes to a portion of the body
that has gone astray—errors
of the hand the heart the mouth the eye.
Before bed, a slow exercise
imagining to sleep each contiguous
part and part and part till the whole
body is offered within the dark
sleep of a great fish and spat
out where the sea transgresses
the littoral, where the shore
connects water and land.

Blue Vitriol

for Rabbi Manny Viñas
"I am hereby writing this…for the sake of proclaiming the sanctity
of the Torah."

Do not tell me it is written
I have no right of return. It is not.
Not with a virgule
Not by a virago
Not through a viremia
Is it written. It is written
Sometimes with a virgule
Often by a vav-of-reversal
Always through a mordant
Of gall and vitriol: oak apple, flower
Of copper, lamp black, acacia senegal.

You draw from a dampness that consumes
All, where black birch straddles the air
Over long gone nurse logs, where the sign
Of the Name is ever cycling decomposition
Generation to generation, where the new
Wasp leaves the marble pocked and round shelter
To drift on the wind. And you record with a turkey feather
The voice of the unspeakable Name eternal.

November Prepositions

Into the fog, across the fog, within the fog,
from the winter fog
of Central Park I brought you
out of me and stood in this same hospital,
before this same view where now
behind me you sleep drugged and tubed.
Near nine years you were lent to me.
Beyond, I won't imagine, can't release you back
during this year—I've lost too much
along the path—
under my grief for that dead friend
without whom I live confused, perhaps, as
through Ravenna's November fog Dante wandered
in his exile. His phantoms swirl
around a mosaic, San Vitale fights
against direction, and so he suffered.
From that sorrow, and from fear and grief,
from vengefulness, he made a simple proposition:
between above and below, between in and out,
toward a beyond we live,
up to our necks in this momentary fog.

Waiting For The Lost To Come In Dreams

It hasn't happened as often as I thought
it would, when my first, my Bubby, wheeled up to me
and rose from the chair she'd never had in life,
and, halting with the strain before she fell,
said she understood I needed to know
that everything was ok, and it was.

The lost ones rarely come to my nights,
all feverish now, dank and wet. A trompe
l'oeil or le coeur, apparent shallowness
against the bottomless crevasse
of a Llotse face, its white-blue
ice, a blue like the sky's confusion
of waves and particles bending, coloring
the light, the air, what is, and what we hear.

Blue Branching

after Michael Mazur

In the family tree, Mendelian crosses, human genome sequencing.

In the river mapping the history of what it has transported.

In the blue lines far below the granite plateau of fissures,
past pink quartz and feldspar, to the defoliated vista

Where the river's blue flashes white and grey,
where the blacktop roads flash blue and grey
in the distorting heat linking the arteries.

There was a doctor rushing to work early, tired,
worn, likely, tanked on something, hitting an oil truck.
Both smashed into the support walls of an overpass,
wedded in the welded wreck, the flames so hot
the steel of the interstate itself melted.

It was with another heart, one that slowly crimsoned
all, that I would take my type "A" person
in a metal coffin to the nation's blue-medallioned
arteries, fighting road rage and the urge to grab the club,
by placing a puppet on hand, wondering about the ones
whose portals closed, whose cold feet wrinkled
on the threshold, whose arteries failed, blocked, broke
down quivering out of rhythm, out of rhyme.

A seventy-five-year-old man stopped at a speed
bump and accelerated into my great-aunt, breaking
her aged bones, tossing a fatal clot

into the demented courses of her system.
She never wanted to leave Chelsea, its rivers of people,
the way it returned memories of arriving from Russia,
her mother swinging a blue tea kettle over
the trolley tracks. Don't hock me a tchaynik
with the future. This is the river we are in,
are in now, she meant. I step in it today, and today,
and today it carries me, diverts or carries me.
When our blood is empty, I know, it is blue.
And when our streets, or rivers or lives are empty, blue, too?

Aunt

How do you know if you are hearing the tea kettle
about to whistle or if the hoarse breath
that forces itself up as withheld energy
is also the whistle, the whistle before it becomes sweet.

And of the runner's false start on the track—
someone sits with headphones, watching the machine signal
a lifting off the blocks after, but too soon after
for human possibility, the electronic starting pistol,

its sound like an answering machine's
notice of messages.
What we expect, what we come to expect
what we have learned.

My mother taught me that blood matters
and *she* taught me that it didn't.
With the fierce unacknowledged competition
against my uncle's family, came a no, a not-us

masking as critical judgment. And it was just
movement of neurons from viscera.
Was the unanswerable, unreachable ideal,
the difference between eating flesh slaughtered

ritually, salt-drained of blood,
cooked to the un-chewable moment
that repeats this is my people,
and a rare sirloin steak pink and dripping.

How can I tell if she loved me despite who I was
or because of it, if her liking me
mattered more than her loving me, if her open
pleasure in me cut the riverbed of my present grief

years ago or if her hasty departure hacked it away
now with such astonishing force.
In the final hours of her life
we watched what might have been her soul

sinking and rising and sinking again
within a light coma
while the fingers said everything
the way they dug into my cousin's flesh

or into the sheets, the way they ripped
at the wires and tapes, the IV, the finger monitor
so what we saw was her and was also merely
the body.

And what about crows, the way they have been
known to solve problems,
what about those crows of New Caledonia,
the ones which plan their tools

and build them so, the hook and the step-picker,
without fingers how they pull grubs and ants
for their meal, the way each
colony does it differently from each other

and the same,
the way that this combination of cognition and style
is what we call culture, and what we never thought
possible is continually being made somewhere.

Is Ephraim A Delightful Child?

"BROTHER, Stop that right now!"
(Shout, alarm, a first burst of coherence.)

But the electric razor didn't stop
Mowing. Carelessly.

Determinedly. But my father
didn't stop razoring. Carelessly.

Determinedly. The face of his baby brother
lay on its body in the hospital bed

in hospital pajamas stained with hospital
soup, sheets with tinctures and bile.

Rachel weeps for her children wailing
bitter weeping and the Lord

brought him back. He slapped his thigh
and was ashamed. He made his confession

holding the hand of the confessor
and when the words finished, all was yearning.

Because of this vision, when I woke up after I saw
it, my sleep was pleasant to me.

Hey Diddle Diddle

With his old world manners he kissed
my mother's hand, chomped on his fractional
cigar and paced the narrow Charlotte Street
apartment to the rhythm of the radio's
violin concerto. My uncle
was still an undergraduate
in physics at CCNY,
my father teaching physics,
and they observed their cousin Fritz
Mandelkehr, whose Viennese
degree in civil engineering
(pre-stress concrete) vaulted him
over the Shanghai oil company
which employed him during the war,
and over Georgia Tech
where he touched down
in the late forties,
vaulted him over the moon.
What a cow he had! He knew
just enough to misread Einstein
and "prove" him wrong. His book,
A New Theory of Relativity,
had received a polite
dismissive letter from the man himself.
Mandelkehr's formal
clothes were unwashed.
His shirttails hung out.
Beside the depression-glass dish
his spoon dripped tea
on a stack of sugar cubes.

How can I transcribe the accent
of the Austro-Hungarian empire?
The way my family scattered
themselves across Europe
and then were moved again
and again across borders
in great muddled migrations and murders?
The way they recorded their affection
for Kaiser Franz Josef in the memory
of how he once waved
as his train passed the edge
of their Ukrainian town?
Or how he entertained, Solomonic,
some local dispute? Can I transcribe
their loyalty, the way they calibrated
their disbelief at all that fortune
had flung them? Transcribe
the redness in Mandelkehr's face?
The exact pronunciation
of the phrase he repeated
all that post-war fifties afternoon—
Aynshtayn Ees Eh Kreemeenall
Aynshtayn Ees Eh Kreemeenall
(Einstein is a criminal
Einstein is a criminal)?
The way those little dogs laughed?

Acknowledgments

"You Take An Onion" grew out of conversations with Raphael Sugerman, whose award-winning series, "Asthma: The Silent Killer," was published in *The New York Daily News*.

The quotes in "Winchester" are from *Chronicon Richardi Divisensis de Tempore Regis Richardi Primi*, edited and translated by J. T. Appleby.

For their careful attention, I thank the editors of the following publications: *Barrow Street, Blues for Bill, Greensboro Review, Inertia-Magazine.com, mamazine.com, Michigan Quarterly Review, PoetryNet.org, Salamander, Southwest Review, Stone Canoe, Sunscripts, Too Darn Hot, Triquarterly, Yale Review, Zeek*.

I thank Adelphi University for the luxury of a sabbatical leave and faculty support grants. Thanks to The Corporation of Yaddo, The Virginia Center for Creative Arts, The Eastern Frontier Society, and the Saltonstall Foundation for their gifts of time and space. Thanks to the Bronx Council on the Arts for a BRIO fellowship, and to *Michigan Quarterly Review* for awarding "Misericordia" its Laurence Goldstein Award in Poetry.

Thanks to Mark Jarman and Kate Daniels, who read this book in early drafts and provided invaluable advice and support. Thanks to the editors of GenPop Books for their enthusiasm. Thanks are not enough—but will have to suffice—to Philip Alcabes who sustains everything.

About the Author

Judith Baumel is a poet, critic and translator. She teaches at Adelphi University where she was the Founding Director of the Creative Writing Program. A former director of the Poetry Society of America, her poetry, translations and essays have been published in *Poetry*, *The Yale Review*, *Agni Review*, *The New York Times*, and *The New Yorker*, among others. Her work is represented in a number of anthologies including *Telling and Remembering: A Century of Jewish American Poetry*; *Gondola Signore Gondola: Poems on Venice*; and *Poems of New York (Everyman's Library Pocket Poets)*.

Her previous books of poetry are *The Weight of Numbers*, for which she won the Walt Whitman Award from the Academy of American Poets, and *Now*. She attended The Bronx High School of Science, Radcliffe College (Harvard University) and The Johns Hopkins University Writing Seminars. She lives in The Bronx.

More info: http://www.judithbaumel.com

Available from GenPop Books

Judith Baumel, *The Kangaroo Girl*
Michael Klein, *then, we were still living*
Julianna Spallholz, *The State of Kansas*
Alan Semerdjian, *In the Architecture of Bone*

& the online magazine from GenPop Books:
No Contest

www.genpopbooks.com